MONU-
MENTALLY
MAD®

#72

Edited by John Ficarra

WARNER BOOKS

A Warner Communications Company

Once, not too long ago in our galaxy, we were invaded by a movie called "Star Wars" . . . and it was so spectacularly successful that it led to further exploits of "Star Wars" such as posters and dolls and toys and jewelry and coloring books. We feel that it's only a matter of time before we are assaulted by the ultimate "Star Wars" spin-off . . . namely, a musical based on the movie. With this in mind, let's look into the future, as the Editors of MAD present . . .

THE FORCE AND I

THE MAD "STAR WARS" MUSICAL

ARTIST: MORT DRUCKER   WRITER: FRANK JACOBS

*Sung to the tune of "Cabaret"

ARTIST: MORT DRUCKER   WRITER: FRANK JACOBS

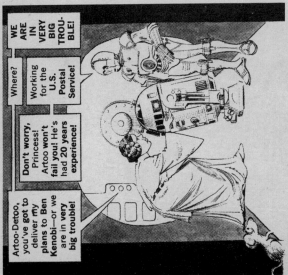

But I was hit in the head . . . and you bandaged my FOOT . . . !!

I'm ALSO rather senile!!

I'm Ben Kenobi! I drove off the Sand People when they attacked you, then bandaged your wounds! I'm an old warrior who's rather clever . . . !

This one's a bargain from southern Polaris—
Takes out the garbage and cleans off your terrace!
If you're neurotic, he'll read up on Freud!
That's what we've got in a second-hand 'droid!

Here's a cute number who's called Artoo-Detoo—
Tagged at a price that you're sure to agree to!
Give him a home and he'll be over-joyed—
That's what we've got in a second-hand 'droid!

When your workers
Join a u-nion—
And they raise their
Fee—
Just flick on the switch
Of your second-hand 'droid
And you'll get your work
Done free!

*Sung to the tune of "Do Re Mi"

*Sung (briefly) to "By The Time I Get To Phoenix"

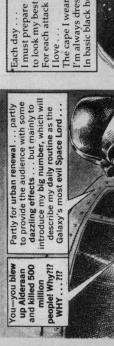

You—you blew up Alderaan and killed 500 million people?!? WHY....?!?

Partly for urban renewal ... partly to provide the audience with some dazzling effects ... but mainly to introduce my big number, which will describe my daily routine as the Galaxy's most evil Space Lord ...

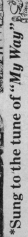

*Each day . . . .
I must prepare
to look my best
For each attack here!
I love . . . .
The cape I wear—
I'm always dressed
In basic black here!

I then . . . .
Put on my mask—
I have it shined
Each week on Friday!
And this . . . .
Should tell you how
I'm starting
My day!

At noon . . . .
I have a meal
Of molten lead
On shredded granite!
And if . . . .
Depressed I feel,
I wipe out dead
A passing planet!

Each world . . . .
That's blown to bits
Can turn a low
Into a high day!
And this . . . .
Should tell you how
I'm spending
My day!

*Sung to the tune of "My Way"

*Sung to the tune of
"The Windmills of Your Mind"

This is See-Threepio! I'm not at home right now, but if you leave your name and number at the sound of the beep, I'll get back to you just as soon as I can . . . .

We rescued the Princess, and now we're trapped in this garbage pit!

Don't worry! I'm phoning See-Threepio for help . . .

Boy, I hate phones—answering machines!!

Now I'm on this leaky space-ship
Where for me there's no escape,
With a greedy, gung-ho pilot
And a screaming 10-foot ape,
Plus an adolescent kid who's
Never seen the Milky Way,
With a robot who keeps beeping
And a 'droid I think is gay.

And I know I'll meet Darth Vader
And soon after that I'll die,
And I'm thinking on the whole
That I prefer the River Kwai—
And I wish I could unwind,
But I find I'm in a bind
'Cause the Force
    Controls my mind!

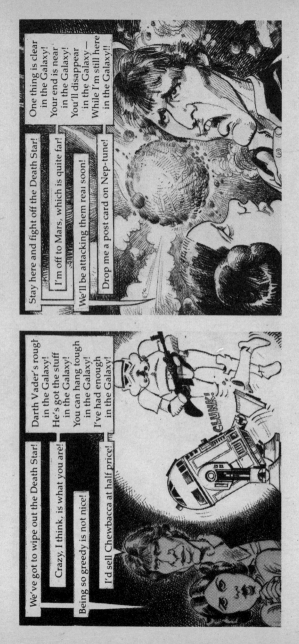

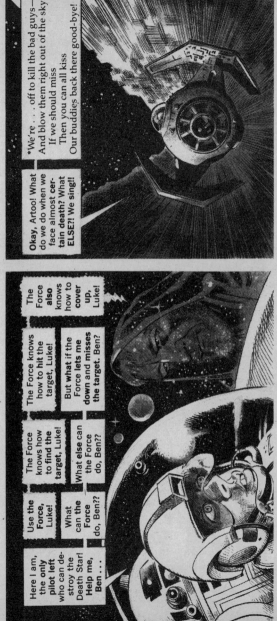

*Sung to the tune of "We're Off To See The Wizard"

We've grown accustomed
   to the Force
That pulls in people
   to this show!
We've grown accustomed
   to the gross—
No other show comes close!

We're big! We're hot!
   A smash . . .
      we've got—
   we've got
With tons of
   money pouring in
From fans who
   make our profits grow!

Although we could have
   killed Darth Vader,
It was not the
   thing to do!
We'll need him in the
   future when we
Bring out "Star Wars II"!

We've grown
   accustomed
      to the clout—
The way we
   all made out—
Ac-customed
   to the
Force!!

*Sung to the tune of "I've Grown Accustomed To Her Face"

ONE EVENING IN AN AMSTERDAM BUS TERMINAL

THE LIGHTER SIDE OF...

OVER-RE

ACTING

ARTIST & WRITER: DAVE BERG

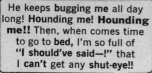

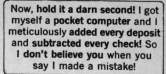

Why restrict the awarding of medals to the military? After all, Civilians perform heroic acts while fighting life's daily battles as well! Let's recognize them with

THIS ISSUE'S PROPOSED
MAD
MEDALS

. . . TO BE

PRESENTED

TO DESERVING

CORPORATE

EXECUTIVES

ARTIST & WRITER: AL JAFFEE

THE BLACK LUNG MEDAL

Awarded to Corporate Executives for outstanding service to stockholders in protecting their annual dividends by effectively avoiding and delaying the installation of those costly, but much-needed "anti-pollution devices."

THE NO-FRILLS
PRODUCT AWARD

Presented to Corporation Executives
who display noteworthy ingenuity in
cutting costs of manufacturing their
products by reducing the quality of
workmanship in them . . . thus avoiding
having to raise prices to consumers.

THE HANDOUT OF
FRIENDSHIP MEDAL

For service above and beyond the call of any corporate duty—by brilliantly disguising campaign contributions and cash gifts to legislators in order to influence votes favorable to the company in any matters that may come up.

THE FRAMMIS AND
GRIBBISH AWARD

For brilliant achievement, consisting
of introducing colorful made-up words
into Warranties and Guarantees, thus
affording the consumer an interesting
language experience, even if he does
not actually understand the meanings.

THE DISTINGUISHED
FLYING MEDAL

Awarded to any Corporate Officer who courageously makes use of the Company Jet to fly to a major sporting event, and then writes it off as a business trip . . . so that every taxpayer helps pay for it, not just the stockholders.

MAD NOVELTY ITEMS FOR PRACTICAL-JOKER JOCKS

ARTIST: JACK DAVIS   WRITER: PAUL PETER PORGES

LOADED, NON-FLIPPING TOSS-UP COIN

FUNNY FALSE TEETH MOUTHPIECE

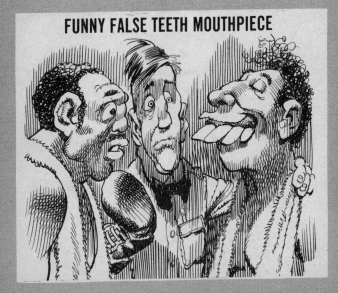

SHREDDING CHEERLEADER POM-POMS

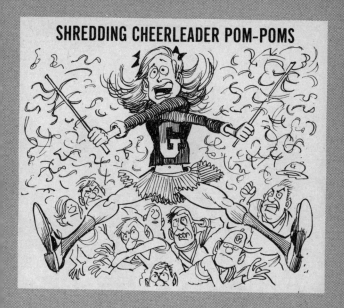

SILLY-PUTTY HOCKEY PUCK

NO-EXIT FOOTBALL JERSEY

REFEREE'S SOAP BUBBLE WHISTLE

BLACK-SPOT FAKE GOLF HOLE

TRICK STARTER GUN

NON-BOUNCING BASKETBALL

WHOOPEE CUSHION SECOND BASE

DOUBLE-SHPRITZ SQUEEZE WATER BOTTLE

EXPLODING RELAY BATON

COLLAPSABLE POLE VAULT POLE

SQUIRTING FENCING TARGET

FAKE BASKET-STUFFER'S FINGERS

HUMOROUS PIT-STOP FLASH CARDS

SPY vs SPY

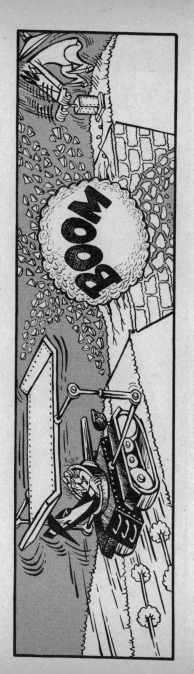

There are a lot of changes going on in the automobile industry these days. Unfortunately, Detroit's advertising hypes remain pretty much the same—as lavish and exaggerated as ever. Let's take a look at a typical new car ad:

EXPERIENCE THE RIDING COMFORT, THE LUXURIOUS APPOINTMENTS, THE STUNNING STYLING AND THE ECONOMICAL PRICE OF THE NEW

1979 FINSTER FIREBURNER

Sounds great, huh? The problem is, you can't drive the ad! Now, let's see

HOW TO READ A NEW CAR AD

ARTIST: GEORGE WOODBRIDGE   WRITER: ALEN ROBIN

● GETS 35 MILES PER GALLON ON THE ROAD

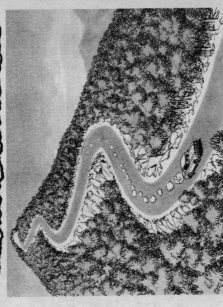

Sure, if it's the road down from Pike's Peak, and you coast.

● POWER BRAKES: STOP CAR GOING 60 IN 30 FEET

Unfortunately, they can only stop the driver in 40 feet!

● MEETS GOV'T. POLLUTION STANDARDS

Standing in the showroom, yes! But just start the engine!

● 15,000 MILE FREE SERVICE GUARANTEE

You'll use most of those 15,000 miles going back and forth to the Dealer's shop to replace the parts that don't work!

That's right . . . if you push this hunk of junk off a cliff.

If you shift to neutral and let the traffic push you along.

● TREMENDOUS LUGGAGE SPACE

If you include the back seat after you fill up the trunk.

● INTERIOR SOUND SYSTEM

Unfortunately, most of the interior sound is engine noise.

● RIDES SIX IN LUXURIOUS COMFORT

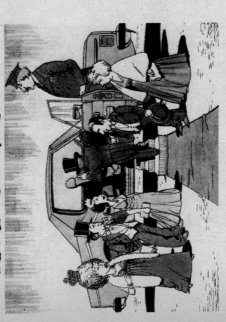

That's true . . . if the six happen to be luxurious midgets.

● INTERIOR CLIMATE CONTROL

The windows have handles inside which raise and lower them!

● RUBBER BUMPERS

These are just great, if you happen to have a rubber back.

● CITIZEN-BAND RADIO

You can use it to chew out the salesman who sold you this "lemon" while you're waiting for the tow truck to arrive.

ONE

AFTERNOON

ON THE
BEACH

JAW'D, TOO

ARTIST: MORT DRUCKER

WRITER: DICK DE BARTOLO

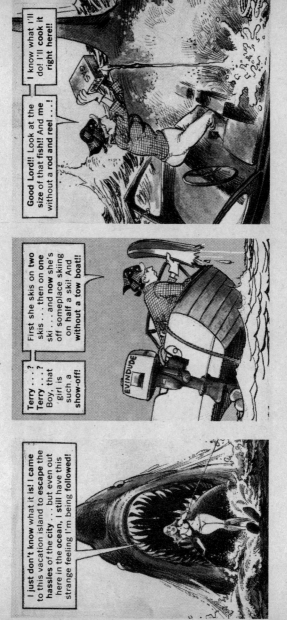

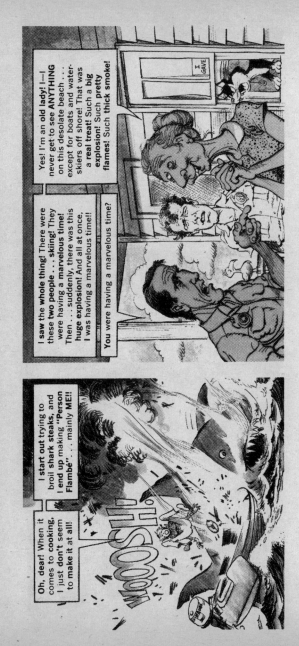

Dr. Elkhorn, I called you here as soon as the kids found this whale corpse! It's obviously been attacked by a huge shark!

Chief Broody . . . I am a member of the Scientific Community! To us, nothing is obvious! We deal only in facts! After examining the wounds, all I can say with any authority is . . . this whale was attacked by SOME BIG MOTHER!!

What would bring a huge shark like that into shore?

They like rhythm! Anything with a systematic beat! They're attracted to drumming . . . solid vibrations!

In that case, why call them "Great Whites"? "GREAT BLACKS" seems to fit better!!

Doctor Elkhorn, do sharks ever communicate? I mean . . . if one shark is killed, could another shark want to take revenge??

Sharks don't take things personally! However, as far as taking revenge is concerned, if I were you, I'd be very careful to avoid anyone who paid good money to see this disappointing sequel!!

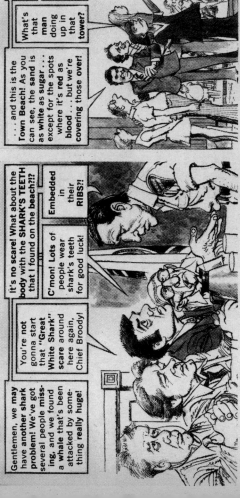

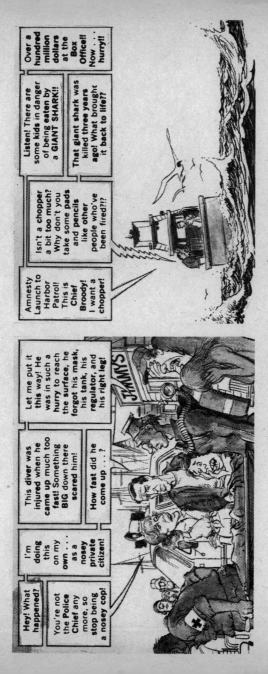

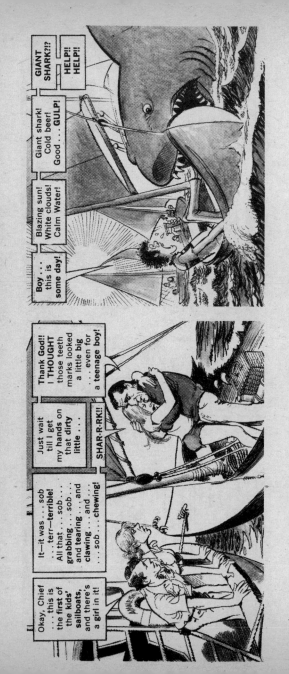

CRASH!

The only trouble is, that shark is **SMARTER**! He's moving out of the way . . . but fast!!

It **IS** a boat, and Chief Broody's at the wheel!! He's real smart! He's going to try to smash right into that shark!

If you were **EVER** going to ask that question . . . this is **NOT** the movie to ask that question in!

Yeah, and it could be a **SHARK!!** Who ever heard of a shark with a motor?!

Wait! I hear a motor! It—it's coming this way! It could be a boat!

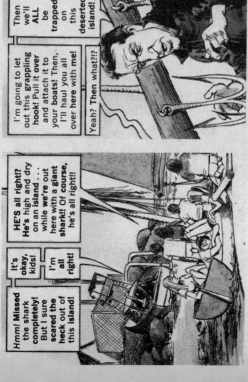

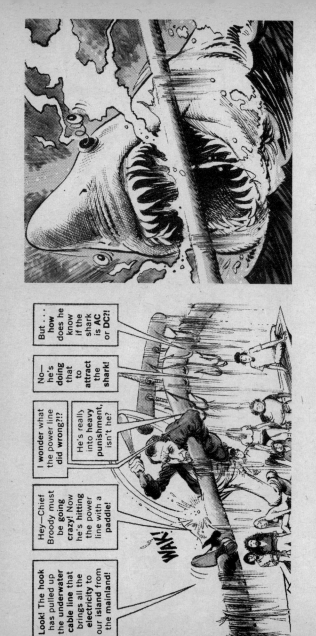

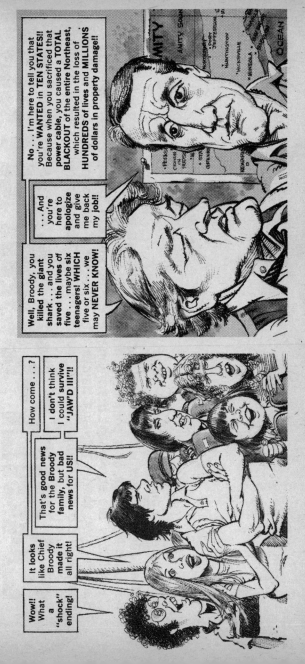

During the past few winters, weathermen have been adding insult to injury by not only telling us how cold it is, but also informing us of the "chill factor" . . . which is the equivalent thermometer temperature—plus—the wind velocity. But why stop there? Why not devise other "factors" that apply not just to the weather, but to year-round "human" conditions? We'll show you what we mean with

EASILY-COMPUTED

HUMAN FACTORS

ARTIST: PAUL COKER, JR.
WRITER: DENNIS SNEE

Your...
MASOCHISM FACTOR

. . . the number of years you insist upon remaining in that big city.

+

. . . the number of problems you face each day living in a big city . . .

=

Your... GULLIBILITY FACTOR

=

. . . your confidence in politicians and campaign promises they make . . .

×

...the number of promises that they actually *keep* after they're elected.

Your... SELF-DECEPTION FACTOR

=

... the number of Paul Newman and Robert Redford movies you see ...

+

... the degree to which you fancy yourself similar to either of them.

Your...
INFATUATION
FACTOR

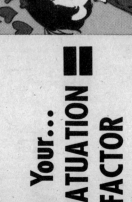

... the ease with which you overlook your new girlfriend's skin condition

... her ability to disregard your certified repulsive personality.

Your... NAIVETÉ FACTOR

... your trust in the oil companies – that announced a critical gasoline shortage just a few years ago . . .

✕

... the amount of gas which appeared miraculously when the price doubled.

=

. . . the number of sexy "Charlie's Angels" episodes you watch on TV.

+

. . . the number of cold, hands-off, unaffectionate girls you date . . .

=

Your...
HORNINESS FACTOR

... the amount of work you do in order to avoid the work you avoid.

...the amount of work you avoid...

Your...
LAZINESS
FACTOR

. . . the lowly social status of the "loser" you actually show up with.

+

. . . the amount of bragging you do to your girlfriends about which football player will take you to the prom . . .

=

Your...
HUMILIATION FACTOR

Your...
CURIOSITY
FACTOR

=

. . . the number of times that your husband works late at the office . . .

+

. . . the number of lipstick stains that you find on his shirt collars.

... the time it takes your smoker's hack to subside in the early morning.

×

... the number of times you've read the surgeon general's warning on the daily pack of cigarettes you smoke...

=

Your...
STUPIDITY
FACTOR

ONE MORNING IN A BUS TERMINAL

In grade school, you probably learned—and promptly proceeded to forget—that bees have 12,000 eyes...that's some turtles live to an age of 150 years...that the heart of an elephant weighs over fifty pounds...and other marginally useful bits of information that came under the heading of "Interesting Facts About Animals." But did you know that there are equally amazing facts about human beings...especially American Human Beings, that rival the oddities of the animal world, and that these come under the heading of "When An Editor Is Desperate, He'll Print Anything!"? Read on, and you'll see that, although a reticulate python may go to a length of thirty feet, there's no length to which we at MAD won't go for an article like...

AMAZING FACTS ABOUT THE ANIMAL WORLD

VS

AMAZING FACTS ABOUT THE AMERICAN SCENE

ARTIST: BOB JONES   WRITER: DENNIS SNEE

Digger wasps derive nourishment from such unlikely sources as *aged tobacco, mustard plasters* and *cowhide products.*

Americans derive nourishment from such unlikely sources as *Twinkies, Ding Dongs, Yoo-Hoos* and *Cheetos.*

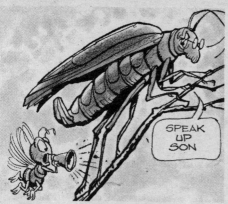

The *ears* of the *katydid* are located just below its *knees*.

The *brains* of a *bigot are* located just below his *wallet*.

An *insect* with its *head* cut off can still continue to *walk*.

An *elected official* with his *mandate* cut off can still continue to *talk*.

The *wolf spider mother* carries its *young* on its *back* until they are able to take care of *themselves*.

The *American father* carries his *young* on his *back* until they are able to take care of *themselves*—and *sometimes longer*.

The *boll weevil* does about *$20,000,000 damage* per year to United States *crops*.

The *drunken driver* does about *$22,000,000 damage* per year to American *life and limb*.

Chameleons can change their *colors* to match their *surroundings*.

Politicians can change their *colors* to match their *surroundings*...only *faster*.

The *May fly* has a life-expectancy of *one day*.

The *luxury sports car* parked on a *city street* has a life-expectancy of *one hour*.

An *elephant* can eat *350 pounds of food* in *one day.*

An *American family* can *waste* 350 pounds of food in *one year.*

An *ant* can carry more than
six times its *own weight.*

An *American consumer* can spend
more than *six times* his *own income.*

Everywhere we shop these days, we see products with the words "NEW—IMPROVED" printed all over them. But after we buy these products and start to use them, we find that the only thing that's "new" and "improved" is the higher price. Which is new and improved for the manufacturer . . . but how about us consumers? MAD thinks that it's about time there really were products that are new and improved. And so, we've gone back to the old drawing board, and we've come up with these marvelous

"NEW-IMPROVED" PRODUCTS THAT REALLY ARE NEW AND IMPROVED

ARTIST & WRITER: AL JAFFEE   IDEA: BILLY DOHERTY

NEW—IMPROVED PACKAGING

Anyone who has ever tried to tear a transparent wrapping from a product knows what an impossible job this can be.

New—Improved packaging contains a small CO_2 cartridge enclosed within the wrapping which, when dealt a sharp blow, fills wrapping with gas until it finally explodes.

NEW—IMPROVED TUBE DISPENSER

Regular tube dispensers of toothpaste, paints, ointments, pastes, etc., are frustrating because the last drops are impossible to squeeze out, which means a waste of money.

New—Improved tube dispenser has cap at each end, making job of squeezing out those last drops easy and effective.

NEW—IMPROVED TOOTHPICKS

Toothpicks can be pointy little hazardous spears when they are accidentally poked too far in an effort to remove glop.

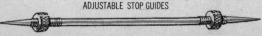

New—Improved toothpick with adjustable stop-guides allows user to safely control the amount of tooth gap penetration.

NEW—IMPROVED KETCHUP BOTTLE

Shloop

Today's ketchup bottle is an infuriating thing that either gives no ketchup at all, or all of it at once . . . all over.

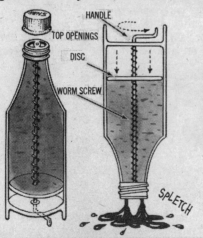

HANDLE

TOP OPENINGS

DISC

WORM SCREW

SPLETCH

New—Improved ketchup bottle has a built-in winding device that delivers exact amount of ketchup exactly where you want it. Handle in recessed base of bottle turns worm screw rod which pushes a disc, forcing ketchup out of top openings.

NEW—IMPROVED JAR TOP

Regular jar tops often stick, requiring super strength to open. This is especially frustrating when you do not have a jar top wrench, or some such tool to make the job easy.

New—Improved jar top has a built-in fold-out handle that provides ample leverage, even for stubbornly frozen lids.

NEW—IMPROVED BALL POINT PEN

Regular ball point pens run out of ink without any warning at the worst times, like when you're taking an exam, writing a check or sending an important life-or-death message.

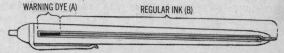

New—Improved ball point pen has warning dye (A) at end of ink supply, which is colored differently than regular ink supply (B). Thus, when the regular ink supply runs out and writer sees warning dye, he knows he has just enough left to finish job at hand, but he must get refill afterwards.

NEW—IMPROVED LADIES WATCH

Most ladies watches are disgustingly dainty and small . . . making the telling of time by them impossible, especially when light conditions are poor or eyesight is failing from advancing age.

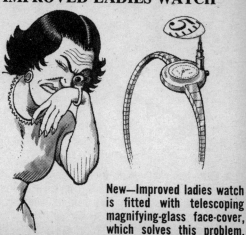

New—Improved ladies watch is fitted with telescoping magnifying-glass face-cover, which solves this problem.

NEW—IMPROVED EYEGLASSES

Slipping eyeglasses is a very common and vexing annoyance. New—Improved eyeglasses have snap-on head-yoke that stops this problem once and for all. Mix-and-match decorator styles and colors add a touch of elegance and excitement.

NEW—IMPROVED PAINT BRUSH

Cleaning a paint brush not only ranks as one of life's more unpleasant jobs, it also seldom gets done right.

100% CLEAN BRUSH

HOOK HOLD UNHOOKED

SELF-CLEANING UNIT

HOOK HOLD

New—Improved paint brush cleans itself. Brush is made with attached self-cleaning unit. When hook holds are opened, cleaning unit is held in one hand while sloppy brush is pulled through its powerful squeegee rollers.

NEW—IMPROVED TEA BAG

Regular tea bag has string and tab attached for dunking into hot water. But often, tab and string follow bag into cup, threatening to make tea too dark unless it's removed.

New—Improved accordion-type tea bag opens easily to stretch across top of tea cup, eliminating chances of falling into steaming water, causing embarrassment as it occurs, burnt fingers when you try retrieving it.

NEW—IMPROVED GOLF BALL

With golf balls becoming more and more expensive, losing one is of serious concern to most golfers. But millions are still lost, no matter how hard golfers look for them.

TRANSMITTER MOUNTED ON SHOCKPROOF SPRINGS

BLEEP-BLEEP-BLEEP

New—Improved golf ball contains tiny shockproofed solid state transmitter. Golfer with receiver easily follows his personal signal (each ball broadcasts on a different wavelength) until he locates his ball. Miniature battery lasts a year, and broadcast range is one mile. Any golfer who hits his ball out of range would be glad to lose it.

NEW—IMPROVED POSTAGE STAMPS

Regular postage stamps contain foul tasting glue that is often ineffective, causing stamps to fall off during mail handling. With today's Post Office policy of not delivering mail with postage due, many problems can and do occur.

New—Improved stamp is made with peel-away backing. This not only eliminates disgusting task of licking the yecchy glue, but it also provides an adhesive so strong that not even rain-soaking the envelope will loosen the new stamp.

NEW—IMPROVED ENVELOPES

On many occasions, mail recipients do not have any letter openers handy, resulting in mutilated mail and cut fingers.

New—Improved envelopes contain string tabs much like the ones found on "Band-Aids". Letters open easily and neatly.

NEW—IMPROVED BOOK MATCHES

Regular book matches are torn out, used and thoughtlessly discarded, causing messy conditions and even fire hazards.

New—Improved book matches are attached to elastic strips. User simply stretches one out, strikes it, lights up and then lets it snap back inside its cover. When all matches are used, entire book is discarded, eliminating messy job of picking up individual burnt matches, plus fire hazards.

ONE HOT AFTERNOON IN THE AMERICAN DESERT

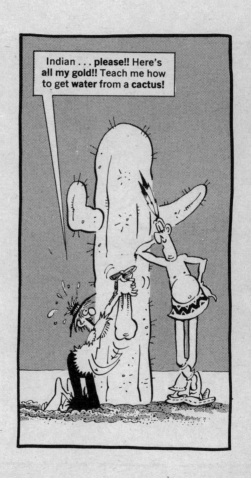

THE LIGHTER

BOO-

SIDE OF...

BOOS

ARTIST & WRITER:
DAVE BERG

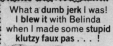

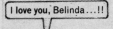

EARLY ONE MORNING DOWN IN SOUTH AMERICA

SOME IMAGINATIVE MAD SUGGESTIONS FOR...

RECYCLING YOUR THROW-AWAYS

ARTIST: AL JAFFEE   WRITER: PAUL PETER PORGES

EMPTY TOOTHPASTE TUBE TOPS

can be used as cleats to convert
an old pair of sneakers into...

TRACK SHOES

AVOCADO
PITS

can be dried
and used as

PRACTICE
GOLF
BALLS

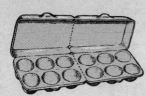

EMPTY EGG CARTON
can be used as a . . .
CONTACT LENS
HOLDER
FOR A LARGE FAMILY

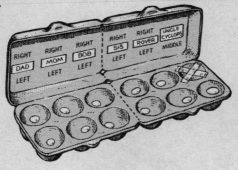

RIGHT DAD LEFT
RIGHT MOM LEFT
RIGHT BOB LEFT
RIGHT SIS LEFT
RIGHT ROVER LEFT
UNCLE CYCLOPS MIDDLE

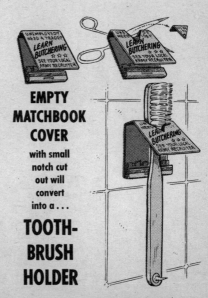

EMPTY
MATCHBOOK
COVER

**with small
notch cut
out will
convert
into a . . .**

TOOTH-
BRUSH
HOLDER

CARDBOARD TUBE

from finished roll
of toilet paper
makes an elegant

BUD VASE

FOR SEDAN CAR

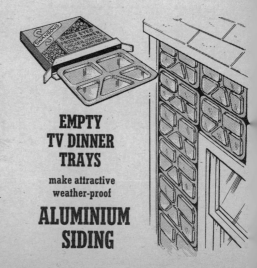

EMPTY TV DINNER TRAYS

make attractive
weather-proof

ALUMINIUM SIDING

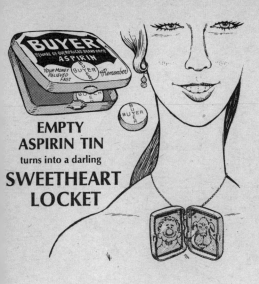

**EMPTY
ASPIRIN TIN**

turns into a darling

**SWEETHEART
LOCKET**

**EMPTY
FILM CANS**

can be used as a
matching set of

**LIQUOR
PONIES**

OBSOLETE TRAINING BRA

used by young
Jewish-American
Princess turns
into matching

YAMULKAS

FOR HER WEDDING

Choking IN THE Sea

PACKED IN SPILLED OIL

LIDS FROM
EMPTY CANS

can be
turned
into
attractive
original

FOLK
ART
JEWELRY

SINGLE SOCKS

left from pairs put
into washing machines
can be used as colorful

GOLF CLUB
COVERS

ICE CREAM
STICKS

can be cut
to proper
lengths for
replacing
those lost

COLLAR
STAYS

SPENT
TRANSISTOR
RADIO AND
CALCULATOR
BATTERIES

CAN BE USED AS
MATCHING SET OF

DUFFEL
COAT
PEG
BUTTONS

LOSING LOTTERY AND
PARI-MUTUEL TICKETS
make perfect pre-cut

KITTY
LITTER

When you think of sea disasters, you think of the "Titanic", the "Lusitania" and the "Andrea Doria." But ABC-TV has added another name to that list of ill-fated launchings. And we call our version of their "see" disaster . . .

LUST BOAT

ARTIST: ANGELO TORRES   WRITER: DICK DE BARTOLO

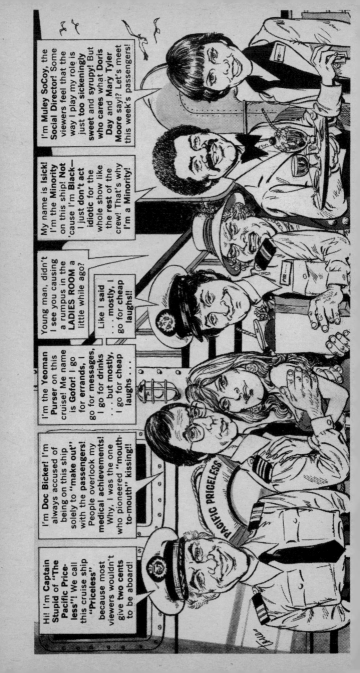